PUBLIC DOMAIN

Also by Gil Ott:

Maize (Pentagram, 1979)
the children (Tamarisk, 1981)
Ladder (Spectacular Diseases, 1983)
Traffic, Books I and II (Singing Horse, 1985)
For the Salamander (Slash & Burn, 1985)
within range (Burning Deck, 1986)
The Yellow Floor (Sun & Moon, 1987)

PUBLIC DOMAIN

Gil Ott

Potes & Poets Press, Inc.
Elmwood, Connecticut.
1989

Acknowledgements:

The poet thanks the editors of the following magazines, where some of these poems originally appeared: *Central Park*, *O.Ars*, *o-blek*, *Pages*, *Panoply*, *Paper Air*, *Reality Studios*, *Red Bass*, and *screens and tasted parallels*. Also thanks to the Ear Inn, North Star Bar, Painted Bride, Small Press Traffic, and Video Box, where they were first performed.

This publication is partially funded with the support of the Connecticut Commission on the Arts, a State agency whose funds are recommended by the Governor and appropriated by the State Legislature.

Cover design by Janet Shimshock.

ISBN 0-937013-29-3

I am calling forth a poem.
I am calling forth a poem.

Come help me sing the song.
Come be with me the poem.

In darkn

When your eyes
to gain's distracting
blur the fearful
pull of your mate past ease

strain on the road hope
that place your mind only
accomodates hemorrhage

sweet to the edge or ignorance
potent dulce
grips the wheel, to yourself
reddening

may ask the cause
of your trouble

within the germ
a tear, strange to you and past
your thin
nerve driven.

Introductory

Language accretes, and molds itself around the precipitant moments of a culture. Where there is cause for celebration, it emerges specific, even ritualized. Where doubt or shame, it covers up and reproduces rapidly, scrambling for the right terms, on to its own complicity.

Poets are born into an acute awareness of these facts. In the United States, our relation to the dominant culture is defined by production of — or our abstention and criticism of — contributory linguistic ornament. The activist role is discouraged for the poet, and it has, today, in the US, atrophied.

Where poetry is permitted to lead, it heals. The poetic processes of attentiveness, association, and performance, overlay essential mental, emotional, and bodily functions.

But the poet's alienation is severe in those societies where the processes of language are cloned and the clones promoted by controlling institutions to rationalize or conceal racism and genocide, or to cheat working men and women. It is a primary task of the poet to question and, as times demand, to challenge such authority. Working men and women are, after all, the majority consumers of language, insatiably so when we are denied our complementary creative, language-making role.

Fortunately, we are not often jailed for our poetry alone in the US, though we *are* jailed for our activism, that is, for our eloquence. Control over the interpretation of language characterizes the true sources of commercial, religious, military, and legal power. Until each new linguistic meaning and form is catalogued and cast as artifact by someone in this crowd, the respect it receives alternates with the suspicion it raises. And America has shown its willingness to act against the writer whose work remains a threat.

Tutored on a consumerist model, those writers in the current American literary community who sense their own failings are offered security in the essentially economic formula: profession = marketable commodity. Personal style, association, and theoretical dogma figure as the professional writer's capital, and accomodate this retreat. Of course, it is to the literary community's credit that it shelters the articulate victims and refugees from the debacle. Yet in America and Europe, the literary community as a whole makes up a class, and it does harbor charlatans.

Language is no one's. Never was. The true site of all language is in the pairing, writer to reader, speaker to listener. The poem is public event, host to a multitude of private entries, a defined anarchy. Understood and practiced in this way, it is powerful.

The regimentation of meaning is criminal, even in the least increment. Language is at once ambiguous and persuasive enough to offer itself as a tool to advantage and oppression, and seen as medium, neutral. Complicity in this crime, as auditor/actors as much as speakers, contributes heartily to our public experience and behavior, as consumers, workers, citizens.

The poems in *Public Domain* are antipathic to such complicity. They should be spoken aloud, and they should be heard. Look for their author on the street, driving or walking, at work, thoroughly exposed. Look to yourself.

LEVELS ADDRESS

Why start with a self-reflexive question? The imperative levels address. What I have needed, simply to get off, is that illusion of form address implies. The bi- or multi-polar, talking to.

One hour from now is waiting. What anxiety inheres, wants out, to bud. So much behavior, between us, fixes our suspicions. But I have tools to make an index.

I am satisfied with very little. Dusk begins my day and continues in lengths, undifferentiated. Write neither of, nor substitute, to keep you, reading. After all, honesty is only custom, or better, custom is custom. Each full page waits against argument, then, taken from neglect, asks questions.

Watch what falls from this tree. Step up and shake. Name's ________________________. Was that mine? Come closer.

Observe, speak. Inequivalent in method, but essentially questions. Always letting one out, then sorting fish. What is the gesture for breadth of acceptance? Once you start interpreting things, it's hard to stop, and who's to say you should? A man arrives with a big white sheet; the ice gets thicker. Think of you think of yourself.

What current language is available to us all, a gloss and pitch, more than its freight determines commonality.

How many are you? I write a letter to the one I love best. Some write back, but never really does. Love wasn't the idea.

Finding the time for many receipt, as, consolidating many to one, times harden. That is difficult. Compose, be calm. Theft takes a steady hand, and patience. How many are you, hear me?

Neverminding what's said, is intransitive implies you. Take my advice. Questions, toasts, confessions, suggestions... lead. To me. Look at it from my point of view. From consensus hums like a house, or other pleasant-sounding logic, always plain. Get by the neck and think it.

Remember my days in what show fluid. I anticipate yours, suggest a beat. Look at yourself. An agreement we rewrite. My currency in yours, grace.

We are concerned
each
with you on your flight
art accustomed to one moment
only me. That you have committed
act independently,
redundantly to yourself.

Strength
a prayer work fecundate
alone, a footprint, two
won't hear. We send
slip into an envelope conceived
outside our text's
necessary reference.

Lord, speak
these difficult
in our hands fragments value
that you will commit, to raise
child, precursor.
Small faith
take.

He'd left her a note, tomorrow.

Chance precedes a shudder, which pops on before dawn. Venus, weak by comparison, is drowned in the difficulty. Light in his eyes, blinding him, hubby piled up his rig, tied up the highway. Past harbors, harbors examples. Without means, the shudder keeps running. She snaps the lead.

"The problem with him
insistence, with no need to answer any questions. Person unnecessary, address diffuses. I can report to you that he. Started in mid-step, he ran. We might erect a fence, or just suggest limits, arbiter. Either way without a doubt.

You'd by what I call necessity, by what's inherent. I want to go back from the light in my eyes. I might make it a narrative's already done. The project

Talking around
that's hungry at the site of me. A rich foam satisfies my inhabitant. Today, to buy a chance on tomorrow. Talk of origins; talk of names. Equal mine ever, like I'd bought the goods he claims he never offered.

In on it's complicitous, gnawing inside. Am rhetoric could kill the speaker, taste of blood like copper. Ate my fingertips. Greed, the object, 's words untutored from a mouth. Sick. Knocked out a tooth.

But let's get next to each other. Call me by my first name. What's your pleasure? Are you comfortable here? Will you need me for anything else?

(having
left
a question
in the odor of gas

my
heart accelerated
down my

wanted relation
to a substance
worm

can't
turn you loose. Anybody's guess assumed a map of alien terrain. Willing, but stupid, the spirit, to. Filled my throat. Knob off in my hand the door swung open, and I shoved reflection

to a holding. What choice? These days I liked to raise the image of my obsession to an in on party. He has his own intentions. No room for the infirm in agreed behavior.

A part of net when isolated, otherwise taken out of love. Buy into electric, then unwind. Stay clean. Transgress. This competitor is mine; hold him, it, in me. The parapet diminishes, I think, then stepping over it, wake to pain.

Ignoring the word in me. Male to persevere, an enemy in gestate overcome. I'm bored through to the wall, violated, by a language making so much fucking sense to me. Conceived in heat, which suckers thrive in a loaf, in a basket? Attack 'em pell mell, they divide your efforts. What drum at a maggot.

The freedoms
of the addict
comforts
what
I'm talking about into
any skull whatsoever
its own fever
to a row of palms by fire from behind the conflict
lit adolescent glory, a chosen,
a long drive chewed through dominance.

Host to refinement needing definition in blood let
strapped a foregone mix to dispel pain. Introduce
a toxin seals the solution keeper kept
off an acre's capability, its requirements
exhaust the hostage.

The struggle in blue, for allopathy, narrative holding out for dawn. Upped the ante plays it big on opposing flanks, all bulk without detail. Anthem through a powder hole to your own thoughts, if you've got any.

Care for a knot

bled tissue vales to call a domicile, mistaking
aperture's phase. Tending kin

to my old
muck
the willed
arrest
damned
exhalation
mirrors

Yellow Field

for analogue
sets a comma
to planed wood

marking a
you for my
periodicity

burns, and how it
wrecks me
revives me

gone to the furthest
outpost, grain
to take a name

wed
alcohol to wood the chalice
broken

force
detected
damned initial

like a blade flies
to disregard
tenders demise

'd mirror & mirror
constituting
stands a place

atop an image, music
pressed from several
sides

with me returning
means distinct
contention

gloved
at birth or birth
assuming eminence

on histories
exaction
tax transgress

a pinprick in a poem
bring
that brick down

LONG

Each evening's banked
clouds at an altitude to drive

the question home. No counting what
brings torpor on. Models topple

unresolved and the road not taken, taken,
stinks. Salmon on blue, she's stretched

before her invitation fails in headlights
or a head throb, doting on minutiae

in the way of my dust. The pronouns
deceive, been legion, but my practical

testing middle age demands one even
as rules go to play. Take her,

for instance, trussed but ambiguous figure
of speech, a mental image eager

to serve. Think of it and roam,
swerve. Eyes on the road.

WHITES

to tell it
calm and quietly
starved of my
owner

habit to gloss, tossing her hair. Wants blocking wants her woolen pleats, her silk. Grace among needs to impoverish. Look! A draw that know myself awkward and premature.

Declined's active, rejected passive. Hop a slot where people live like roaches. Choices of sexual idiom tack me to another post. But each has his use. Squeam a little here, a little there, soon everyone knows you. And you are abundant, available

to the market for albums, magazines, tobacco and alcohol. She's no fade. A pastime of suffocate clears dreams for seductions, leaves soot. Cherry, Cherry, out all night, shopping.

Too many matinee idols pile my lost opportunities in the sink. Later never comes. Out that window, in the field behind the house, further, bought

tickets to vicarious
battery
vents captain's
pent anger

dulled by conflict. Hunger obeys. Want a blow job? The servant dips and scram enforced nightly. Customs flourish at the bal du siecle, ringed by caliber. Ladies and soldiers remain loyal to form. There within the out back a nuts jungle piously spreads his legs. He applies the iron. That sack of bones is closer to the Lord than I. God sort 'em out. Buffalo nickel, Indian head penny, tender wood limb acquiesces, turned their propaganda on themselves.

Abraham came out of the tall grass, pale from fervor. He gave the workers the day off, and sat there by himself. He'd had a vision of the future (this is not one of his more famous exploits), determinist linkage and auto-trans, damning, never doubting himself. Were ovens

affecting little
bait to jail

stamina, limited, furious. Expect to bulge, dye in the carotid artery. White knuckles, Rolls of whites

edged the woods. I'm going in under cover. The treaties are a crock of shit. My cattle were took, and mine's downriver to heathen. I'll need help.

Combustion engines outside, electric motors in. Bits of powder bits crosses an information line otherwise numb. Keeps progressives on their toes. Rude to organize suicide you

capacity
to turn them
erotic
conflict

Went up her moving image. I saw to it twice, until it left. Some distributor's desire to exploit saturation to a tissue. He wants a buck. He minds his business.

Serially fixate broke off at the turn in the road, onto a convenient billboard, but spilled as well, sinking in. Sneaked a chocolate. Ha ha! You're home early!

congruence and plenitude

remember who I am at any moment. Resisting returning. On a shelf in the second of those rooms, something I've made rests. Paper and clay uncertainly. Now I want to test the man on the phone, at the counter, my desk. You and I listening hear the similarity. Multiply

the determinant
act preceding insight, from that dark gradually
your face, and then, as if into myself

repeatedly and without distinction.

Talking about
the violence in the act, how plain expression accumulates a code. I want to touch and you, to be absent. The pauses, countenance, become perfect alum. The pauses

privileged to talk about loving you. The rest of the language is out on strike. Who will replace the woman never correctly thought? The question is wrong, but one of intention. At what point has she retreated?

Strange to judge a man, dancing with him. Too loud to talk keeps them from me. We need this formality for practice, simulating in the mood. I like to keep my thoughts short.

I asked him when the machine would be free, the whole day so a month or year, a coin in my mouth. He's at the controls, profile, full view, identifiable. I hate the model to the real thing, who's just turned away again.

sex of the air, my
hips
mind behavior alone among books
fine
to achieve notoriety
set
that tree to that rectangular
heat

pays on receipt
keeps his thoughts to himself. Remember the guy in the red suit? Downpayment is a disease like any other. A habit. Keep your eyes on street level, off folk, there's goods

occupy affection. So shoot me. There's no law says I can't

impersonate

fellow professionals. Pornography in the age of mechanical reproduction. Reproduction itself. Hip to axle, spoke of water rising to a well. The skin like a rubber tarp, pulled over it, wave register.

When
symmetry in two lines
and a gap between

enough
past into myself waiting
for him at the door

omit my black
skirt, the look she never

business
done in there.

itch at watch
against a corner

stockings midthigh
to the hem

wormed
leather

case lightly in his right hand. Shoes as thin transmit the stone's texture. Linoleum stings. Under his arm the forty-seven postures boxed estimably. "As if heat had to be invented!" he laughed, at tomorrow's meeting

pulled his chain. The girl is not pretty. Address the men, one woman in suits, as arranged. Beat the hell of a tight sock

sober to bruise
were no more children
to garter

nailed or pierced the little web abandoned, and he flushed. He wept. Temperate pressure a balls corona, the blood pushed back and pushing back. Bonded

aggress waiting for the light to change. Clock her neck from the street upstairs to strap and ride, appointments waiting.

lost another year
that pads the girl
up, down, in and out of view
toughs it, ignorant, took one around the corner
in some
doorway.

place violated by an early dusk
trusted what device a man installed
against enduring,
the hard breath up at noon
's boiler to accompany me
to bed at any premium.

smell th'polyurethane's aged and brittle
past weight, light out under my scalp as I go
down, fume and trash
on entry only only answers myself
talking
followed me home.

lost
footing a mouse's shadow followed
th'exact curve, a man no bigger out
my side wriggles and tugs brown liquid
crenellate the stub's remaining
vengeance, resists.

small threats under appurtenances mine, draw kinship
out multiplying signs, actual voices out
of synch
spun, drop, accelerating, pierce one

unremarkably, with this fist opening and any
grit mixing

as unified.
A house cat's sniff about shit congeals it.
Keep else's fears to reading, Hand,
attend and recognize these
leaves fallen
on no dead.

Yellow Field

notion of driving
head, or slats
to a wall

that overlay as over
vapor
of the fur

torn in an eye
from cover
came an accusation

she'd
me darkly
whisper

past a mat prohibited
descent
grasses

hatched, divided
talling over
dirt

from angles indiscriminately
spread
a figure, copula

illuminate
a gesture
will without

you
privately
blood

transgress
along a fir branch
quivers

drops
as dropped
into complexity

the subject
liquid
seeping

The forgotten

wound may be too great to finish telling. No source to it, the illness moves. Every object blank when I am looking in my mind among injuries. The poem to think. Better of coincidence of a sensory world shunned the acid.

The red out of the cat's mouth proud you a sucker to your face. Hit his hat hatchet job on you've worked for, despair of. Class of violence wants the very rocks off that hill. Chase him down a crease, onto the street and under a truck. Under and gone.

Alive tolerate the equivalence of your pain. The Miskito in the way, the Mayan, in Salvador, Atitlan, you're done for playing along. The price you pay or get out.

I've made terms on put the hemo, coil in solution up-my-sleeve wheeled to a poorer neighborhood. A chorus of hard comparison. Out every brick vault grew disoriented to took ambulatory, sharded out, away from me, out.

My hand more than my eye, as it passes over that primitive, coded
pattern, more of soil

streets we knew

walk with you.

The stores and houses in a regular grid are more than silent, and meet their excess with a silence

in need of any verse agreed tacitly to imbue. Its fabric, like a map, needed us, or, later, me alone, and tolerated my control. Memory's the ruse. Present value translates not into labor but that theft

glass from sand to condemn

abstract. This money represents an

paradox revealed only in the loss. I see a weft to the line of poplars. Your house is on the right.

This is the way a dream dispels pain. It, too, draws from a store

out there alone. A material simulation says the same thing. Or a new friend. The heart mismanages

tactile share. The garment's scarcity means both poverty and wealth, we attribute to its makers. That you carried that cloth equal to the translation

it lost what I had already denied you.

She listens to the radio while busily tones her flesh. Hum time of day, of industry, as every day her movements brush her nipples on her shirt, she bends to sweep. Were there sudden rain it wouldn't fill more space. Dark atmosphere and light, warm and chill contending. Unique, proudly at work condensing the countertop.

The defensive stance has the worries the vehicle, who only a moment ago thought herself a machine. Spite is possible to be happy, grinding it out. Vulnerable to cheer concedes from in or out a muscle, or a muscle system resolve to count coin. Push a thigh, bowels, nausea.

She hasn't tired of syntax, driving, or what's to come. Make it up, and add to this addictions defrays late clarity. Surrounded by disorder needs a blood gluepot, touches herself, nearwinged. Pauses. Continually the plains, the preparations meet, surround, subdued, pass into memory that is, for all her elasticity, a window elsewhere.

Twelve lanes compress to six behind the row of houses opposite.

Blood pooled in her calves, her thighs and back when her fertile button popped. Voices through the wall, the girls next door, a cried in a rented room. What's residual, the walls confused? Heaved stiffened. Then she turned and brushed his buttocks through the covers, intentioned and unreasoned.

Her step on that loose floor board wakes him.

Night everywhere but here. I come in to counteract discomfort. The eyeball for bloodshot, finding it, ashamed. Choose retreat over quizzy, Jack's accident scene. His phallus, this body. In a noise grate sends me wander lonely, to me, myself. Stores on stores, and clouds above a silhouette dad talks mom away. Be be be baby. Came potted meat weight, of the arms hung from clavicle, spine to mat, for freedom. Dad to momma tap tap tappa tap tappa tap — I'm dancin'! Till fatigue and otherwise cool, ambiguous groin. Thus fertile. A primer little more than no explanation.

She to all women I to she. Plane to wood a square of moonlight taut: a logic. Twelve interior edges, but to one the palindrome to me hushed.

Who put the bolt spins from her far galaxy. How her body knows so little save when toddled trusts her own devices. Has learned today osteo-isolate to break a posture, to change tomorrow. The several means to accede, spread a mat, to split. Slumps.

The glass moves a pinpoint familiar to a field out of spin.

"Of her weight, although she didn't physically lean on me. I'm at the machine, typing, and she's standing behind me. Make me nervous!

"I'm telling you, or somebody, not my old boss in the hallway, to a rattling of peers.

"Thoughts that cut another shorten me. Came to cry, addled Becky not yet on's conspirator unwavering. Too much latinate following no letup from the phone subdues me. Next undergrad moves up, my neck stiff, my sub on break. Tired. Tired of articulate."

Learning to cross more than filigree out to reading each day singly, a world.

Puts on, her coat. A confidence about a comment scores the marriage. Tarns of them Catholic girls count for less. Julia scolds the neighborhood, but it's a bad night's sleep, traffic to come heads her tongue. She returns to sweet on him, the vestibule turtling up with her in it still. A moment. A parting. Breeze portending rain toward her car.

Let the problem draw it close to recedes. Fits like a hat. The rupturings a more appropriate pronounced her loins in determining tides. Doubt to surer politics, braking downhill. None of it's easy. Half past last spotted.

to Julia's hand

Due to the tensile swift
at an edge dispels

around my waist, or any circle you
and I determine utterance, what's in

performer to an intimate grasp, locked
lightly

your failing fails of its disclosure.
A random confidence the apprehension

tests a gate, opposable
as ancient teeth, tongue, thumb and index
absently count. Alternating in
and out and wanting
all in the fuse reiterated, yet to injury
exposed as scarified, grip deferring

a life of service along the serrate
fin confluent to the brookside.

Expressing what's difficult
strands you've worked
or daily meet, what comic
parrots necks of a wrist

from intimacy subject to intimacy told me
quick I'd owned in sentiment only, vertebrae neatly

separated and, too full a portion, fallen.
Out of precedent, unfitting, never saw
sent on what wire, you hold my

signals, thoughtfully in check. You are cool,
a little damp, mine. From every far

accretion
palm to absolve
it tested

quietly, holding the pen.

Radicalism

Before gone requiring a stronger vehicle. Reach pushes into the dry soil doesn't emerge. Emerge continually, you plow and dissolve true radical.

Before names passed and is standing over us in which tree, by this message, collecting bits of mineral to petrify. I'm singing to the past up there marching, brutally tricked and not to my illusions. History in telling without asylum peace in the blood, tyranny in language.

given
under sycamore. Applied it came to me like an idea. Curl in rust. I have worked and worked to this grain collectively, whose

deaths inform a stroke of filing, filings lining up. The goal: seamless effort. Keep from freezing with a song, in turn, from memory's duration

overturn deceit. Con-
flated deci-

material
from ash re-
trieved

a visible flame. Planed wood tree reassembling, so from bone,

friend, my vocabulary spreads, pales at senses. My shadow in shade. Carry

sack of others'
compositions; no

matter, they'd'a ate
your family.

Get
bit. Limp. Mix

wisdom with dirt. Don't
be too obvious

when you talk
to fish.

(... Names never wrote but laughed. Thinking, once the movement of my branches, out of text or accomplished. Difference is past here. Trace, chart a course, its source in the present that's the sound of leaves at the end of summer, clatter.)

How come to terms with a comfort volume control a visitation phantom selects? My method has gaps, ignoring me? Whose program the beginning but unending staccato conceives in ruts (a word), troughs (waves), anger (silence), and none precisely.

Parent educates veils a threat. The difficulty of starting a leg up in the grave. Settle down. Heard any jokes, the late cynic ecology continues to gnaw, better than me, than most. Processual to rot her downstairs alone in bed, watching TV. A man to answer to. A vulnerable man. A man's hand aging, twitching, etched and untrustworthy. God love the bugs are hit and flying.

Between you and me, whose perspective fits description? Tied a ribbon on that tree, there. The dye ran. Name became the name of name exaggerates to strangle lesser senses. Then damned if the mind don't start to go.

Caught rubbernecking. Transit toward a wood, first memory, without effort. To an alley offers comfort. The people near wiped-out deny myself food. Lakota, side of the highway. A leg off in the story. The irrelevant versioning possesses so much land strung out.

Either way, I've got the best microbial surface. Think about it a trilling bird sings, it's sunset! That swelling, that dream about disease subject, to take care, predicate. Fucking commas, catch my feet.

In that heat whose purpose felt the pull of muscle over bone? Hard work the body's fall wouldn't want, got took by the sun.

Up in heaven I was attested by bees bright yellow and *indifferent to me.* A friend held one foot, a rope around my neck, I took my first step. The earth would not record my weight. Past then the men broke voices in me, matter-of-fact, I wanted one or many. To this day my hips are numb, and slur my speech.

Story my decay, my life. Given to pleasure choices a swollen finger kids to its relent in stupor. Dialogical with the end predicted, a truth. Syringe cause of the trouble. Laugh at the rush in my temples, the heat engendering a spin. How political is hunger? I wrote a clue for my time tomorrow, flickering painlessly.

Accident of birth asks I seek a violent end tutored eyes on else. The lord's indifference hot potatos it from that scene, or needn't, the sanctuary built on swamps. Some serve. I drove the car into the tree, Officer. You see a dry need; I'm otherwise incapable.

Past dignity
to we who disbelieving formed a ring
the smoke shot through the grass
bellowing

in its simplicity
pure hell closed 'round
a hole in the night.

What's known reposite what cannot be mentioned. Two of me. One in the pit, ill, the other peeling leaves away.

The surf is organized, yet tired slate that works for everyone. With no thought containing the work of sleeping, conflict, which among children is a badge won out of danger. But such risk earned pushes a thought past thinking. Nausea. The loving hand familiar's lost its blood, falls. Never done move on to something else.

attack had put him back in the hospital. The tape ran out, so I didn't get his number. Calm, Bill's face before me, difficult friend, but in the urgency I felt in dialing the hospital's main desk to get it, friendly duty. He may die, that's clear. Write it down. Thank you. Hang up. Hesitate

the same themes I'd called escapism always, and usually tried to avoid when he and I talked. The elusive teaching job in Fiji, a return to Wales, to Aberystwith, where he once taught for a year. This time I encouraged, welcomed fantasy as a real option. "I have a test on Monday. A catheter, man." Just getting home, where he was alone, lonely, cooking himself a meal, would be enough. "They put it in through my neck." Desperate sentiment. I've felt it, too, on news from the doctor. Sought more distant return. "Whatever they tell you, Bill. It's not the life

choses
safely right of the line a forward
collapse, another display, a more real
bid for succor. Transient
ends to gobble
how many more of you?
One year, four years, eight, your
dependency spent, love sotted with talk
around next
spring pushing daisies through this old overcoat. The bass line,
too, disintegrated; last bird out of the cave blinds the impatient

to paining's habit deduct regular narrowing
fix on one, desired, each accursed

in writing her down. In negate. In difficulty short years sunk into dirt. We'd dug two pits, much larger than needed, and packed. We've taken poison. A gravity toward I've come into the narrative late. I'm with poison me.

transparence
leaves "like a shower of coins
to move among
communing, to depend

or gain nothing spending water
over fisted creek
my lover's voice, her visage

out of time singularly implored
comforts a poverty
clayed

slips heavy
from its casing. The population
of the world
commences

Yellow Field

One pole strung
with wire on the crest
of a hill. In this light

all I can see.

nothing grows, the legend

cut changes minds, not minds
abbreviated to sell tedium.
Afternoon the Morning contradicts, yet behind it some in-
tention
laws

to piss, to question behavior, to
rise at five to walk to work, carefully parsing verbs
the tribal history in photographs

a hill that rose, rises, perhaps
the remembered color walled
on wall off even
when it rises clear before no one,

the guards
are delicious
inaudible
lyric

for the rest are stories everyone
but me
knows
from the steps where fallen scrip for a rewrite
buys these days? Whatever the have-nots

mumbo-jumbo terror outside town declined
a job in no position, or produced
a story counter to the brotherhood. Justice won't condone a
metaphor. Breaks we give what words to change choose rat-

tles in gunny, weights attached. Restraint, child. Your script's about done. Suit private ideology slapped opinion polls with tickets so the informants, trading ID's an Army helicopter at the treetops, feel our thunder. Wake
up in a cot
sweating
at the typewriter

angels
ring
the letter "P",
the manacles, the grating

lies, I suspect, when spoken
to.

PRIVATE LIFE

To dis-
bridge men to me detach column lines we hook-up daily. To discrete roles at the elaborate cornice, of the antic carved there, on my trade sworn. As a thief sworn among crud where I
would hide my one
true habit
more to shame than its interior
appointments, one
by one and each
more solid
lasts tended out of water. I may lose consciousness, but society continues. Fare time to linger over souvenirs. A kind of property gone to tenements match esteem to clutter. I'll trade sepia vote for higher octane. In this society the old men lead
lean into fire
as the meat
allows. The choice begins come home in a box. Take a number at the door. A job's a job but on your profile over hobby find ability to kill. I'll be tanked by dawn and down to the plant
erased
my neck, what's good
for the country
stamped
grade by lottery
assumed, according to shoot straight mythological hardons six for a buck. Not enough to sell my sex option out of pocket. I may not own the language but the meanings are mine. Whose homogeneity? Fear of the tube to jump cut some emotional
dysfunction
am dying

where I live powerless
to stop my hands
shaking, breath shallow
this calling on its orbit falters. Sow contentment to your sleeve when to the crowded marketplace you balk at history. What reference? What past doing something completely original. Start naming the birds. I'm in this body, door locked, economy, of the illusion.

up short on him
question-like
to avoid traps
advantage the arctic
man or wolf does what he wants
a surfaces
incrementally
all of them a unit moving
there, there
using English on the prow
to generalize
his kind
allegiance be fed
through the teeth
caution
out this stranger's back door
brick yard
foot's a loose
hands wrenching up lugs
cheaply
pried and scattered
members called other stops
on entering
uneasy
talk in the depressions gathered
out of rope
itched
up creek to throw
a sentence
quickly cored
to cacophony's
mazes

trusts accuser's
lip, sect
and depend
indentured

FIGURES

Fix your eyes.
Careful

a characteristic gesture, a tic has soiled utility. Pare off what's intended to the true routine. In this scene shank rests left right left right an idiosyncratic sway to the pelvis like grinding his teeth. What sounds destined's but the next corner, arriving tired.

Figures of production. The terms mean less when used. Listen to the facts pulling a needle through my cloth. Too often short of breath. Fact compacting needle's skill puts to run, a daily threat. Rules to live by

observing any given
through

But I'll embellish what I see, seeing in fact sentiment.

resistance, not as stone, but stone
better left

At the instant of discrimination, at the seed of the rationale, fist over hand. Who holds out his hand? Who's paying? Payment is artifice. Their linkage is linguistic, poverty as well of the same equation. Agreement or violence

Knowing what a knife cut
too keep the place clean

Don't rest. Don't describe. You won't fail but be burned.

to empty
my life

cautious to the last atom
nesia's implied to stay alive

Debunking spiritual poverty as a thing not yet successfully defined, sup with us. Do you know where your next meal is coming from? We're like any company, but better. Who'll say grace?

My can't help comparing mine with theirs. I continue shrinking. I am taller, taller by far. Do you like the way I strut and spit?

Poor

got
his
angry

touched pissed his leg deprived. Common to the victim completes the characterization. Summed for the instrument, run down revving or after work, the mechanics of bubble-packing burned in. One day the man'd

to represent a class. But the boss can't be bought. In our memory

saved a wheel's purpose
between
my hands
a metal
cut

man hours
of making of the oozy glass
vials in obscurity
for the Greater

nods, or nearly does, as from on high, acknowledging his vague imprisonment. He paces in his chair. All of one Good, the machine's a fetter to his arm, an example from a great house to these little tics. He looks directly at me. The condition

dismisses its containment. Orders from semen, from bile and vinegar. From no liquid wrapped in pincers to adopt and overthrow its purpose. Divide and subdivide, and at the end of sleeping,

curls a knuckle down
white street
working off a
cattle prod a gang in-line
devotion

of the attitudes his prayers
are catalogued,
discarded.

Yellow Field

bitter pronoun
lost
a pellet

standing by a given
name
like acid

from the brow
down
an insufficient

figure ground
such pleasure the teeth
permit

from coalescing
shit to eternity
oppose

iconophratry to determination
dies,
another forms, like

excrement
no part
kin to me

here aching
hole
in evil as in water

tamed irony
counts
pulses

off among flies
wonderfully organized
after suicide

combining
in a digit
all that in a pit

confounds
entry
to interior

ferns and mucuous
swell to dull
sense

PROFESSIONAL

extent the fingers
with instruments tests
precise coordination to the job

saving lives, minds
charmed or lost brotherhood
in comparable

soul careers. Ghost
the little attitudes up
from the envelope

times boredom equals
by birth conflicted
prized truce. It didn't

work then nor will
to talk of other than compromise
it later than you think

Stingere

Heat
seeking the remittance
ocorpse on's levied
heavily
door to door-wise clogs
th'exhaust dammy
switched-on middle class
ablowin arap conned particulate
disreputes iheap
up's profits n'exports pollutes
'em outta fruits
labor tunnelling they heirs'
chances used
up atom amode ander
snatch inna oven tooths
jagged be commerce inter
alia buys
another year avoids
s'subject enactor inner
ther sunset fullogrit
fer guy/girl counter pores
outta livin po nasty squeams
the rigger t'be A number one
k'next n'next n'next stampun um
offer xerox gunning exxons
ybloat. Unguent
to legion apply blame
affixed patch at bachy
gearjawin abt bein teed
awhile shunne plants

waging bi-cuts er
wortless shim beem attitude
t'counter pain offolk
ammedic an actuary recollect
per court o'co.'s'side ever
enna bleed
smeared occult off
cited nat'l sec'ty oft
eds til calmed
and spread buboes arrest.
A pin prick enneed manifold
strung to caps
fumes ababes bonfire
outpacing thism's supporate
promises aware sin fluence tobacco
whiskey poor iconography
emmesms whip hour
will to a wire
heat teach uns burnin a taut
scar rapid suck
umbrage wade out sustained
on market day
be crimmen skirmish enaddled
sold ardour
to bussy a fect'l
collapse astride empires
alies greeds many small
pustular ends.

SHUTTLE CHALLENGER

red glare
image enhanced

in awe the nation's payload
plume at 59.262 divergent
yaw and pitch

in air gave proof
bombs
cheer

the military workhorse
throttled up
to milliseconds

lost
for their country in God
Wars

consolidated wealth tooled
up in space struts

Control to see the right solid rocket booster
gleaming

"How many centipedes went under the wall when he came in? Better to pick her up by the ears. When thunder comes in over the hills I feel big, then I feel small. Thirty steps from here to the house. A few more will be alright."

Here, the sunlight like a bedsheet. Arrogance act to know a man, perhaps confide in him, and then to come upon him by surprise, talking to strangers in another language. He is an enemy. Kill him and there will be another, perhaps many more.

"Not my logic. I'm a crocodile. Recognize me? Gnawing on a green twig. A perfect liar."

Watched *Miami Vice*. Had a drink. Took a shower. Got to chill out. It's all in the way you carry yourself. They're hung up in debate. Let's get

Threat of the Good Example. With an average attention span of 11 seconds. Snub out that cigarette; not bad for a gink. I'll make a clock in that foliage. Cut it! Hard it is just to talk. Whose hair is this? It's matted, bloody.

Not a person on the streets, all boarded up, not even a dog. There are no maps and no telephone service. Aim for their accomplishments, their school or granary. No more general talk. Back home they've got all the answers and they're all wrong. This detail feels good, my legs under me as I stand up and start walking.

"The story is she'd been to Nicaragua, and had gotten sick. She'll dance like that for a couple of hours. That was a year ago. Sweating. She laughed, really a full laugh, and then she dropped."

Each comes with his own presumptions. That's a hindrance gunfire drops. Call a doctor. The more you understand, the less you want to come here. And no support from home.

Status

About, within me sounds, metal seizing and releasing
devils knocks a racist percept
off a ledge, the barrio alive over heaving by.
Mine with fluorocarbons, byproduct of a dance
that fascinates me. In its lives of the third
person gratified and hid needy. More needy
came to rob me, picked my
pocket wage I'd traded a wife, little pick
the kid's drug hunger. And I am similar;
the population produced that aberration
in the gut strung for sale.

Midway on the path of cast
lots remembering my name that no guide's
dropped his kindly prod to trust me
loose on any African street, to watch
imagining orders fail to coalesce. Stone
color of lard begs a vandal. Why should I
cut wrists to name an heir as firing layabouts
hacked a city in its sleep. Days each waited
with the rest, wearing nothing, full of blood rubbing
back his chafes. Nights rifle our camps, no harm.

I won't apologize. None to advantage but the spot
price of oil, and exhausted at that
copped this attitude. There's birds in the highway
stick up your wallet, the Bastard, I can see him
almost clear! Then he gets away.

Don't notice we've trench in the Township puddle
of warm and muddy drink with pride
out of my all summer. Divided against
the went down, the way their children
group at the pool, not remarkable, really,
when my neighbor steals and tells.
An armed vehicle leads the water tank.
No, I know it wasn't always so, but so
five died since Tuesday. The president
delirium on its pivot sits like an image
over fuming. Past the heat
distortion three men load a metal chest.

Stink endured a character of its own, increasing its demands
past five. Allowed to club greed.
More propaganda footage turned
with the public ugly, or rather, refined to the same
end, habit, blunt, leader of exiles.
How's the cult? Hold the pill
under your tongue kills fleas like me, Bigshot.
Remember, I earned my money
cables Yalta with a change of plans
advanced wipe out a village. Breaths in a
hole underground, a tin bunker.

Some recommendation, to say I've got feelings
a line of tenements a brickyard
kicks like yesterday's mule. Interior
ex-child takes any blame, a cockroach
from the food chain fixed watching.

Denounce my fragments among and scolding the "conveniences
to pollute a mechanical lens off stage. Put my face there
the plate drops, molded lead.
Damn the fuckers make a profit off it up
prop mustard rain in a ghetto, stay in today.

My wit and my ability compressed to a shovel's
blade against the supple wounded, never
under capitalism boasted these directives
folded, brushed, and laid upon the fire.
Hunger calling talent to fish it up
to an erection. Get it? You
already got off in New York, but hey,
it's a job you say your storehouse
to storehouse of elevated purchase, shooting it out.

Can I trade force, pass it on to an empty
chamber tenant? Inside her stiff at a long
indifferent stretch, becoming money
quick to sterile with the Lord's work.
Silver latent in me, lost
combination of humors rules
the world broke killing me.

I'm not done carving my leg. Not done
proper name's fetus yields
8% drawn and quarter compound
the insult won't give birth. Leave one ink
for another, sicken from that one, leave
it running into the earth at my feet.
I've got nothing more to say. Dig elsewhere.

that is uncompleted, day
to another age my life in a mirror
obeys, as if there were laws to the succession

events not counted in greatness, which greatness,
articulated, is its own vulnerability.

From proliferate
meaning what is behind every tree, some danger
revealed. The pleasure

bring in the first person I see,
at another table, separated from me
by a device. Practice

myself the little wand
arc where ought be sky, burn
awkwardly in love, in trying

POTES AND POETS PRESS PUBLICATIONS

Miekal And, *Book 7, Samsara Congeries*
Bruce Andrews, *Excommunicate*
Bruce Andrews, from *Shut Up*
Todd Baron, *dark as a hat*
Dennis Barone, *Forms / Froms*
Dennis Barone, *The World / The Possibility*
Lee Bartlett, *Red Scare*
Beau Beausoleil, *in case / this way two things fell*
Steve Benson, *Reverse Order*
Steve Benson, *Two Works Based on Performance*
Brita Bergland, *form is bidden*
Charles Bernstein, *Amblyopia*
Charles Bernstein, *Conversation with Henry Hills*
Charles Bernstein, *disfrutes*
Abigail Child, *A Motive for Mayhem*
Clark Coolidge, *The Symphony*
Clark Coolidge, *A Geology*
Cid Corman, *Essay on Poetry*
Cid Corman, *Root Song*
Tina Darragh, *Exposed Faces*
Alan Davies, *a an av es*
Alan Davies, *Mnemonotechnics*
Alan Davies, *Riot Now*
Jean Day, from *No Springs Trail*
Ray DiPalma, *The Jukebox of Memnon*
Johanna Drucker, from *bookscape*
Rachel Blau DuPlessis, *Tabula Rosa*
Theodore Enslin, *Case Book*
Theodore Enslin, *Meditations on Varied Grounds*
Theodore Enslin, *September's Bonfire*
Norman Fischer, *The Devices*
Steven Forth, *Calls This*
Peter Ganick, *Rectangular Morning Poem*
Peter Ganick, *Met Honest Stanzas*
Peter Ganick, *Two Space Six*
Carla Harryman, *The Words*
Carla Harryman, *Vice*
Susan Howe, *Federalist 10*

Janet Hunter, *in the absence of alphabets*
P Inman, *backbite*
P Inman, *Think of One*
P Inman, *waver*
Andrew Levy, *Reading Places, Reading Times*
Jackson Mac Low, *Prose & Verse from the Early 80's*
Barbara Moraff, *Learning to Move*
Janette Orr, *The Balcony of Escape*
Gil Ott, *Public Domain*
Maureen Owen, *Imaginary Income*
Keith Rahmings, *Printouts*
Dan Raphael, *Oops Gotta Go*
Dan Raphael, *The Matter What Is*
Dan Raphael, *Zone du Jour*
Stephen Ratcliffe, *Sonnets*
Maria Richard, *Secondary Image / Whisper Omega*
Susan Roberts, *cherries in the afternoon*
Kit Robinson, *Up Early*
Leslie Scalapino, *clarinet part I heard*
Laurie Schneider, *Pieces of Two*
James Sherry, *Lazy Sonnets*
Ron Silliman, *B A R T*
Ron Silliman, *Lit*
Ron Silliman, from *Paradise*
Pete Spence, *Almanak*
Pete Spence, *Elaborate at the Outline*
Diane Ward, *Being Another / Locating in the World*
Craig Watson, *The Asks*
Hannah Weiner, *Nijole's House*

Potes & Poets Press
181 Edgemont Avenue
Elmwood, Connecticut 06110